Contents

Successful Object Sermons

Roderick McDonald

BAKER BOOK HOUSE
Grand Rapids, Michigan 49516

Introduction

Jesus said, "Let the children come to me, and do not hinder them; for to such belongs the kingdom of heaven" (Matt. 19:14).

Throughout my years in the United Methodist ministry, I often was painfully aware that too much of our religious activity was geared to adults, with too little geared to children. Worship ritual, hymns, and sermons were, and frequently still are, prepared with adults solely in mind.

This collection offers typical examples of successful children's sermonettes. Nearly all include suggestions for objects or illustrations, together with suggested means of developing the central lesson.

It is hoped and expected that busy pastors, church and Bible school teachers, family group leaders, and others will add their personal touches to these ideas and make them truly their own.

God bless you, one and all, as you minister to these "Super Citizens of the Kingdom of God."

Roderick McDonald
Escondido, California

1

Clockwork

Text:

"For everything there is a season, and a time for
   every matter under heaven:
a time to be born, and a time to die;
a time to plant, and a time to pluck up what is
   planted;
a time to kill, and a time to heal;
a time to break down, and a time to build up;
a time to weep, and a time to laugh;
a time to mourn, and a time to dance;
a time to cast away stones, and a time to gather
   stones together;
a time to embrace, and a time to refrain from
   embracing;
a time to seek, and a time to lose;
a time to keep, and a time to cast away;
a time to rend, and a time to sew;
a time to keep silence, and a time to speak;
a time to love, and a time to hate;
a time for war, and a time for peace" (Eccles. 3:1–8).

Objects:

A clock and a calendar

Development:

Do you do things on time, or do you procrastinate?

Do you know what the word *procrastinate* means? It means not doing things we should be doing right now, and putting them off until later.

Sometimes we know we should get our homework done right away, but we put it off until later. And then what happens? Sometimes we don't get it done, or we get it wrong.

Other times we put off chores we should be doing around the house. We say we'll do them later. And then what happens? Sometimes somebody else ends up doing them, because we forget to do them. That isn't fair, is it?

The Bible says there is a right time and a wrong time for everything. To be responsible people, we must learn not to put things off, but to do them instead when they are supposed to be done.

Let's bow our heads and say a short prayer together: "God, please help us not to procrastinate, but to do things when they are supposed to be done. Amen."

2

Excuses

Text:

"The lazy man is full of excuses. 'I can't go to work!' he says. 'If I go outside I might meet a lion in the street and be killed!'" (Prov. 22:13 LB).

Object:

A picture of a lion

Development:

Do you ever use excuses when you don't want to do something?

"I can't go to school today," you might say, "because I didn't do my homework."

Maybe you tell your mom, "I can't eat vegetables, because they might make me sick."

"I can't take out the garbage, because there might be a big dog out there."

Excuses are simply ways in which we try to avoid doing something, and most of the time they don't work very well.

What kinds of excuses do you use? (*Ask for examples.*)

The problem with excuses is that they're often a sign of laziness, an unwillingness to do something that we really should be doing.

That's why the Bible verse today says that the man who is full of excuses is lazy.

The next time we feel like using an excuse, we should stop and think. Isn't it better to do what we must do and avoid excuses?

3

God's Tape Recorder

Text:

"Let the words of my mouth and the meditation of my heart be acceptable in thy sight, O LORD, my rock and my redeemer" (Ps. 19:14).

Object:

A portable, battery-operated tape recorder, preferably with a speaker loud enough to be heard for some distance, and a blank tape

Development:

(Have several children record a few words on the tape. Some may readily volunteer their names; others may have to be coaxed to say a short phrase or two, such as "We are in church," or "This is God's house.")

The psalmist who wrote the text we just read from the Bible knew something very important: He knew that God could hear every word he spoke and could read every thought in his mind.

When God listens to you throughout each day, what does he hear?

When he reads your thoughts, what does he see?

Sometimes all of us have thoughts that we should not have, and say words that we should not say. Sometimes we get angry, for example, and say things that hurt people. And sometimes we feel bad, later, for the things we have said or thought.

What do we need to do about this?

We need to pray and ask God for his help with our words and our thoughts, and we need to ask his forgiveness for thoughts and words that have been hurtful to others. In this way God can help us to become the kind of people that he truly wants us to be.

4

How Much Are You Worth?

Text:

"Then the LORD God formed man of dust from the ground, and breathed into his nostrils the breath of life; and man became a living being" (Gen. 2:7).

"So God created man in his own image, in the image of God he created him; male and female he created them" (Gen. 1:27).

Object:

A handful of soil

Development:

Scientists tell us that our bodies are made up of the same kinds of minerals that are often found in dirt. Our bodies—and many types of dirt from the earth—are made up of elements such as hydrogen, oxygen, calcium, sodium, potassium, copper, iron, zinc, and others.

In terms of ordinary minerals, however, we aren't worth very much. In fact, the value of all the minerals in your body, added together, wouldn't amount to more than a few dollars.

Does that mean we're pretty much worthless?

Absolutely not!

Inside our bodies we have something very special that can't be measured in dollars. God put something of himself in us. He made us in his own image and gave each of us a soul.

So, the truth is, you are somebody very, very special. You're far more than a few minerals. You are an important creation of God.

Don't ever forget it!

5

The Magnificent Magnet

Text:

"Come to me, all who labor and are heavy laden, and I will give you rest" (Matt. 11:28).

Objects:

A magnet, a piece of white paper, and several small metal (ferrous) objects

Development:

(Place the metal objects on the paper. Hold the paper flat, or ask one or two "helpers" to hold the paper flat, so the children and the congregation can see. Place the magnet directly underneath the paper and move the magnet around. As the magnet is moved, the small metal objects on the paper will move with it.)

Isn't it interesting to see how these little metal pieces "follow" the magnet as it is moved, even though they are on different sides of the paper?

Sometimes people are like that, too. The magnet and the metal pieces, of course, are not living, but

16

instead are attracted to each other by their structures and electrical charges. People, on the other hand, *are* living and are attracted to each other and to God by a living force we call love.

Most of us have several people in our lives whom we love. We love dads and moms and brothers and sisters and grandpas and grandmas, and sometimes we love close friends and other people, too. When we love something, we are drawn to it, just as the metal is drawn to the magnet.

Remember what it's like when someone we love holds his or her arms out to us, perhaps to give us a hug or tell us we're special? We're pulled to them like a magnet.

The love of Jesus is a force like that, drawing us to him—just like the magnet. He urges us to trust him and love him and follow him. He is the "Magnificent Magnet," whose love draws us ever closer to himself.

6

How's Your Hearing?

Text:

> "Having eyes do you not see, and having ears do you not hear? And do you not remember?" (Mark 8:18).

Object:

A portable, battery-operated tape recorder on which is recorded a variety of sounds, some well known and some not so well known (for example, the easily recognized bark of a dog, meow of a cat, or closing of a door; followed by less easily recognized sounds, such as the crunch of snow or sand under shoes, hiss of eggs frying, or automated garage door opening)

Development:

(Play the tape, and ask the children to identify each sound. After they've guessed at all sounds, give them the correct identifications.)

We had different guesses on some of these sounds, didn't we? That's because sometimes what sounds like one thing to one person sounds like something else to another person.

18

Moms and dads know, too, that sometimes children are able to hear terms like *ice cream cone* or phrases like *go to the beach* more clearly than they are able to hear *clean your room* or *do your homework*.

Sometimes in life we don't always hear the message that Jesus is telling us about loving God and loving one another. Sometimes we're too interested in other things.

Just the same, he is always speaking to us, every day, through our hearts and our minds, and sometimes through other persons. All we have to do is "tune in" to his messages.

7

Prayer as Incense

Text:

"Let my prayer be counted as incense before thee, and the lifting up of my hands as an evening sacrifice!" (Ps. 141:2).

Objects:

A stick of incense, a match, and a small glass of water (Note: Long, thin sticks of incense with thin wooden "handles" are commonly available and are easier to light and display than short incense cones.)

Development:

(Light the incense and hold it up, letting the smoke rise straight up, just as our prayers rise up to God. Then, blow or fan the scent in the direction of listeners, just as our prayers reach out and affect other people. When the demonstration or talk is finished, extinguish the incense in the glass of water.)

Have you noticed, when incense is lit, how the fragrance quickly fills the air? Because it is available in a wide variety of scents, incense can make the air smell like jasmine or sandalwood or spices or any of several other types of plants or materials.

For centuries many churches have used incense to represent prayer. In the Roman Catholic Church, for example, a container called the censer is used during the Mass to hold burning incense.

Just as the sweet smell of incense touches those in a room in which it is lit, so prayer touches the lives of people all around us. The more we pray to help other people, the more people are touched, and helped, by our prayers.

8

Pins

Text:

"For the body does not consist of one member but of many" (1 Cor. 12:14).

Objects:

A variety of pins of different types attached to a sheet of paper (for example: safety pins, straight pins, sewing needles, curved needles, bulletin-board pins, decorative tie pins, jeweled stick pins)

Development:

(Point to various pins on the sheet and discuss the function of each. At the end of this short discussion, ask the children what they want to be when they become adults.)

You'll notice from our little discussion that pins of different sorts have many different jobs to do. Some hold paper to walls, some hold men's ties in place, others are used in sewing, others are used for decoration, and so on. Every pin has something important to do, even though it may be different from what another pin does. Sometimes the same pin may be used for several purposes, and sometimes many pins are used together for a single purpose.

In a way, pins are like people. God gives people many different talents and abilities, and many different jobs to do. Sometimes one person may have many jobs to do, and sometimes many people work together for a single purpose.

Whatever talents and tasks God gives us, each of us is important to him.

9

Shaping Up

Text:

"O house of Israel, can I not do with you as this potter has done? says the LORD. Behold, like the clay in the potter's hand, so are you in my hand, O house of Israel" (Jer. 18:6).

Objects:

A lump of clay, a pinch pot kept in plastic bag to be displayed at appropriate time

Development:

(Form lump of clay while you are talking.)

Clay is an interesting material. It can be formed into an almost endless variety of shapes.

In a way, we are like clay, too. Just as we can form clay into different shapes and objects, so we are shaped, day by day, into different kinds of people.

To work with clay, we first shape and form and push and pull until the clay is in the shape we want, and then we let it dry. As clay dries, it hardens and sets. After that, it is very difficult to change. *(Display finished pot now.)*

Habits, good and bad, that begin when we are young grow harder to change—just like the clay—when we grow older. If we get into the habit of telling "little lies," for example, soon it is difficult to stop lying.

If we get into the habit of eating things that aren't good for us, or being unkind to certain types of people, or ignoring our responsibilities, or doing other things that are harmful to others or ourselves, these habits soon "harden" and become difficult to break. To break these habits we must stop them when they are starting, before they become too "hardened" to break.

On the other hand, we can work to develop *good* habits, such as kindness, truthfulness, and responsibility, and when these habits "harden," we will be better people and will help to make a better world for those around us.

10

Let Your Light Shine

Text:

"You are the light of the world. A city that is set on a hill cannot be hid. Nor do men light a lamp and put it under a bushel, but on a stand, and it gives light to all in the house. Let your light so shine before men, that they may see your good works and give glory to your Father who is in heaven" (Matt. 5:14–16).

Objects:

A candle and a match

Development:

(Light and display the candle.)

Have you ever been in a Roman Catholic church in which there were dozens, perhaps hundreds, of little candles burning all at once? In most cases these are called vigil lights. They are lit as a devotional symbol. People offer prayers at the same time.

Did you know that each of us is like a candle?

Whatever we do, we are giving off light that others can see.

What kinds of candles are we? Are we bright, cheery candles, bringing light and warmth and kindness to those around us? Or are we flickering, dull, sputtering candles, hardly able to give any light?

Isn't it nicer to be around bright, friendly, cheery candles?

What kind of candle are *you*?

11

He Loves Me,
He Loves Me Not

Text:

"Beloved, let us love one another; for love is of God, and he who loves is born of God and knows God. He who does not love does not know God; for God is love" (1 John 4:7–8).

Object:

A flower with many petals, such as a daisy

Development:

Have you ever wondered if some other boy or girl liked you and wanted to be your friend, but you were too shy to ask them?

Many years ago, people had an interesting way of deciding whether or not someone loved them. If a young man wanted to know if a certain young lady loved him, he would find a flower with many petals, just like this one.

Taking the flower in one hand, he would pull off the petals, one by one, saying, in turn, "She loves me, she loves me not, she loves me, she loves me not," and so forth. *(Demonstrate.)* He would do this until he came to the last petal. Whatever it came out to be—"She loves me," or "She loves me not"—he would assume it was the truth.

Isn't it wonderful that we don't have to be unsure about God's love? We don't need flowers or petals or anything else to help us know. All we need is an open heart and a willingness to let God's love live in us.

12

The Shepherd and His Dogs

Text:

Psalm 23

Object:

A picture of a sheep dog

Development:

Do any of you have a good dog as a friend?

In many parts of the world where people tend sheep, trained sheep dogs not only are good friends to their masters, but they also help guide and protect the flocks from harm.

In the psalm we read, the psalmist was comparing the way God guides and looks after us to the way a shepherd guides and looks after his sheep. We need fear no evil, for God watches over us, guides us, and leads us in the right direction, if only we are willing to follow.

Some people have listened to the part of this wonderful psalm that says, "Surely goodness and mercy shall follow me all the days of my life, and I shall dwell in the house of the LORD forever," and they have suggested that goodness and mercy are like the names of faithful sheep dogs.

We can think about it this way: While the Lord guides us, his faithful sheep dogs, Goodness and Mercy, follow us and help to protect us as we go through life.

No matter where we go, and no matter what we encounter, the Lord is always there, like a good shepherd, to give us strength and comfort whenever we need it.

All we have to do is follow him.

13

Road Maps

Text:

"Thy word is a lamp to my feet and a light to my path" (Ps. 119:105).

Object:

A road map

Development:

Can you find your city on this map? If you look carefully, you will see the name. *(Demonstrate.)*

Have you ever traveled by car on a vacation or other trip? If you went very far, there's a good chance that the driver, maybe your mom or dad, used a map to make certain you went the right way.

People who travel by car or truck use maps to find roads, towns, parks, lakes and other points they wish to reach. If they didn't use maps, what would happen? *(Wait for response.)*

That's right. They'd become lost, and they might never reach their destination.

Have you ever been lost? It's a bad feeling not to

know where to go, or how to get to where you wish to be.

Did you know that Christians use their Bibles the same way, and for the same reason, that travelers use road maps?

Instead of finding a lake or a park or a road, the Bible helps us to find our way through life. It helps us to know what to do and what not to do. It shows us what God wishes us to believe, and what not to believe.

Without the Bible, without that guidance from God, we could get lost in life, and that would be far, far worse than simply missing a road or a park. To stay on "God's highway" we must learn to study and believe the Bible. Are you learning to read your Bible "road map"?

14

Horse Sense
(Palm Sunday)

Text:

"Go into the village opposite, where on entering you will find a colt tied, on which no one has ever yet sat; untie it and bring it here" (Luke 19:30).

Object:

A picture of Jesus riding a donkey into Jerusalem

Development:

Have you ever seen a rodeo?

At a rodeo, some cowboys ride bulls, others rope steers. Some cowgirls race between sets of barrels, and sometimes they have wagon races. Other cowboys ride bucking horses. These horses don't want to be ridden, so they try to throw their riders off, into the dirt.

Usually an animal that has never been ridden or trained tries to throw off anyone who tries to ride him.

In the Bible story in which Jesus entered Jerusalem,

the donkey used by Jesus had never been ridden. You would expect such an animal to buck, wouldn't you?

He didn't. The little animal seemed to know who Jesus was. The donkey was gentle and gave Jesus a good ride from Bethany to Jerusalem.

The children seemed to know who Jesus was, too, even though many grownups didn't. Do you remember what the children did? They spread palm branches on the ground in front of Jesus for the donkey to walk on. That is why we call this day Palm Sunday.

Are we as smart as the children of Jesus' day and the little donkey who carried him? Do we know who Jesus is?

15

Palm Sunday

Text:

"He was in the center of the procession with crowds
ahead and behind, and all of them shouting, 'Hail to
the King!' 'Praise God for him who comes in the
name of the Lord!' . . . 'Praise God for the return of
our father David's kingdom . . .' 'Hail to the King of
the universe!'" (Mark 11:9–10 LB).

Object:

A palm branch

Development:

When you think of a king, what do you think of?

Lots of times we think of a king as someone on a
large, perhaps golden, throne, or someone wearing a
jeweled crown who is waited on by many helpers
and servants.

When Jesus and his followers came to Jerusalem,
many called Jesus a king—but he had no golden
throne, no crown, and no palace. He didn't have
large armies, and his name wasn't on any coins. And

he arrived in Jerusalem on a sleepy little donkey. Still, his followers knew he was a king. They shouted it as he approached the city, and many children threw palm branches in his path.

What's the difference between Jesus as king and "regular" kings who have thrones and palaces? For one thing, Jesus didn't want any wealth or palaces or thrones for himself.

There is another difference, though, that is even more important. While each "regular" king rules only his own country or territory, Jesus was and is called, King of the universe. He doesn't have to have armies or thrones, for he is the king and Lord of us all.

16

Easter

Text:

"Then go quickly and tell his disciples that he has risen from the dead, and behold, he is going before you to Galilee; there you will see him. Lo, I have told you" (Matt. 28:7).

Objects:

A tulip bulb and a tulip blossom

Development:

Everyone knows what this is (*show flower*), but how many of you know what this is (*show bulb*)?

It is a tulip bulb. The bulb is first buried in the ground, and after a while the flower grows from it. How can a flower come out of this bulb (*show both again*)? God planned it and makes it happen.

How many of you know what a cocoon is?

A cocoon is a small, silky envelope spun by several types of insects. It doesn't really look like much at all. Most of the time, in fact, you probably wouldn't even notice a cocoon on a branch or under a leaf. But do you know what's special about some cocoons? Some cocoons, after a while, open up and out of each comes a beautiful butterfly. How can a butterfly come out of a cocoon? God planned it and makes it happen.

Do you know what we're celebrating today?

That's right. It's Easter. And do you know what's special about Easter? God planned it and made it happen. It was on Easter that Christ rose from the dead. It is a miracle—much more exciting than the tulip coming from the bulb, or the butterfly coming from a cocoon.

But Christ rising from the dead was, and is so important because Christ brings us everlasting life. Someday we'll live with him in heaven.

17

Our Spiritual Radio

Text:

"Be still and know that I am God. I am exalted among the nations, I am exalted in the earth" (Ps. 46:10).

Object:

A small, battery-powered radio

Development:

(Turn on the radio, and change rapidly from one station to another.)

This room is filled with radio and television signals, or "waves." We just can't see them. But this radio gets some of them. Some come from stations that are fairly close by, and others reach us from stations that are quite distant.

How many signals, do you think, are in this room right now? Dozens? Hundreds? Thousands? To tell, we would have to have powerful receiving equipment. I think we would be surprised to discover how many signals surround us.

Just like the radio and television signals, God's message of love is all around us. God is sending his message to us all the time. To fully receive his message, however, we have to do as God said through the psalmist in today's text: "Be still and know that I am God."

What things remind you of God? A church? Blue skies? Flowers? A baby? A puppy? A song? A cross? God is all around us. We have only to look and listen.

18

The Perfect Pearl

Text:

"Again, the kingdom of heaven is like a merchant in search of fine pearls, who, on finding one pearl of great value, went and sold all that he had and bought it" (Matt. 13:45).

Object:

A pearl necklace

Development:

Aren't pearls beautiful?

Do any of you know how a real pearl is formed? A real pearl—not a plastic or artificial one—is formed when a grain of sand or some other little object gets lodged inside a live oyster's shell. To protect itself from this irritation, the oyster secretes a substance that forms around the grain, and this substance hardens into the pearl.

For thousands of years people have placed a high value on pearls. They pay large amounts of money to own the best pearls, and they treat them like treasured items.

Jesus said that God's kingdom (his world of faith, love, and forgiveness of sins) is like a valuable pearl. Like paying a lot of money for pearls from oysters, some people give up much in order to find God and his kingdom. They work hard and sacrifice and do all that they can to do God's will.

Do you know what the biggest difference is between pearls from oysters and the so-called pearl of God's love? Our faith in God's kingdom is far, far more valuable than any pearl that ever came from an oyster. Our love and faith in Jesus are worth more than any amount of jewelry or money.

19

Our Magnifying Glass

Text:

"O magnify the LORD with me, and let us exalt his name together!" (Ps. 34:3).

Object:

A magnifying glass

Development:

(Let the children pass the magnifying glass around and look at each other.)

Do you ever get excited about something or someone? Do you ever get excited about a new friend, for example, and want to tell others about this person?

What do we do when we are enthusiastic about something or someone?

We magnify it or him or her. We say things such as, "He is *so* nice!" or "She is *so* pretty!" or "I just *love* the new class I'm in!" We might even say, "It's a *terrific* bike," or "I had a *fantastic* time!"

What do you get really excited about?

How about this: "God is *so terrific!*" We maybe don't say that very often, but we could.

The psalmist in our text today was excited about God. He wanted to share God with all his friends and have them feel excited, too.

We can feel that way, too! God *is terrific!*

20

Courage

Text:

"Behold, God is my salvation; I will trust, and will not be afraid; for the LORD God is my strength and my song, and he has become my salvation" (Isa. 12:2).

"He will cover you with his pinions, and under his wings you will find refuge; his faithfulness is a shield and buckler" (Ps. 91:4).

Object:

A picture of a hen or another mother bird and her chicks

Development:

Mother hens and other birds guide and protect their little ones during the first days and weeks of their lives. When baby chicks become frightened, they run and hide under the warm and protective wings of their mother.

Have you ever been afraid? (*Ask for a few examples.*)

Sometimes when things are dark, or you feel alone or you're not sure of yourself, isn't it nice to have a mom or dad or some other relative or friend who can help to make you feel safe?

In the Bible, when Daniel was thrown into a den of lions, he prayed and asked God for help, and God shut the lions' mouths so they would not hurt Daniel. Daniel trusted God and God protected him.

The next time you are frightened, or about to face something scary, ask God to give you courage. Just like the wings of the mother bird over the chicks, God's love surrounds and shelters us.

21

How Tall Are You?

Text:

"And Jesus increased in wisdom and stature, and in favor with God and man" (Luke 2:52).

Object:

A yardstick or tape measure

Development:

(*Measure the height of one or two of the children.*)

Have your mom or dad ever measured you to see how tall you were? Were you surprised to see how much you had grown since the last time you were measured?

Sometimes our teachers in school use another form of measurement. They give us a test to see how much we have learned, to see if we have grown in our knowledge.

When Jesus was a boy, he grew just as we grow, both in height and in knowledge. Do you suppose his mother ever measured Jesus' height when he was a boy, to see how much he had grown? Do you suppose maybe she made a mark on the wall, and later made another mark to measure his growth?

We know that Jesus grew in knowledge, too. In fact, when he was only around twelve years old Jesus surprised many grownups with the amount of his knowledge.

So Jesus grew in knowledge and in height. The Bible says he also grew in favor with God and man: He was kind, and people loved him.

Although we can't do much about our height except for making sure we eat good food, we *can* grow more rapidly in knowledge and kindness if we work hard at it.

Jesus grew in wisdom and in height and in kindness, and so can we!

22

Heaven

Text:

"In my father's house are many rooms; if it were not so, would I have told you that I go to prepare a place for you?" (John 14:2).

Object:

Picture of a hotel or motel

Development:

How many rooms do you have in your house? How many people do you think could stay there at one time? Some very large hotels in big cities have more than a thousand rooms and a thousand bathrooms all in a single building.

When Jesus was with his disciples and they were concerned about heaven, Jesus told them not to worry. He said that his father's house—by which he meant heaven—is like a big, big house or a big hotel with lots and lots of rooms, so there is room for everyone.

In the Bible it also says (*may be paraphrased*):

And I saw the holy city, new Jerusalem, coming down out of heaven from God, prepared as a bride adorned for her husband; and I heard a loud voice from the throne saying, "Behold, the dwelling of God is with men. He will dwell with them, and they shall be his people, and God himself will be with them; he will wipe away every tear from their eyes, and death shall be no more, neither shall there be mourning nor crying nor pain any more, for the former things have passed away" (Rev. 21:2–4).

The Bible, also in the Book of Revelation (22:1–2), talks about "the water of life . . . flowing . . . through the middle of the street of the city."

Doesn't heaven sound like a wonderful place? And aren't you glad there's room for everybody?

23

Humpty Dumpty

Text:

"God is our refuge and strength, a very present help in trouble" (Ps. 46:1).

Object:

An egg

Development:

How many of you have heard the rhyme about Humpty Dumpty? It goes something like this:

> Humpty Dumpty sat on a wall;
> Humpty Dumpty had a great fall.
> All the king's horses and
>   all the king's men
> couldn't put Humpty Dumpty
>   together again!

We all know that no one can put an egg back together after it breaks. Did you know Humpty Dumpty was an egg?

But, do you know something else? Jesus put many Humpty-Dumpty-type people back "together" again. They thought they had been broken or hurt or lost forever, but Jesus brought them back. He gave sight to blind people; he touched people whose legs were broken and bent and helped them walk; he healed people with bad diseases; and he helped sinful people find God. Even today, sometimes criminals in prison discover the love of Jesus, and he helps them to be better persons.

No matter who we are, and no matter how broken or hurt or sinful we think we are, the love of Jesus can put us back "together" again.

24

Fingerprints

Text:

"O LORD, thou hast searched me and known me!
Thou knowest when I sit down and when I rise up;
thou discernest my thoughts from afar" (Ps.
139:1–2).

Objects:

An ink pad, a sheet of paper, tissues

Development:

(*Put a few fingerprints from some of the children
onto the paper, and wipe ink off fingers.*)

Did you know that no two people's fingerprints
are exactly alike? So, no matter how many people
there are on earth, your fingerprints are not exactly
the same as anyone else's.

Your fingerprints are a permanent identification
mark that belongs only to you. That is why, when a
criminal touches something while committing a
crime, the police can often tell who the person is by
examining the fingerprints found at the scene of the
crime.

In today's text, the psalmist says that God knows all about us, even without fingerprints. He knows when we sit down or when we stand up, and he can read our thoughts.

Although our thoughts aren't always the best, and although we don't always do the right things, God still loves us. He knows every one of us, with or without using our fingerprints, and he gives us his love. All we have to do is accept the gift he gives us.

25

Little Boy Blue

Text:

"And the Lord said, 'Who then is the faithful and wise steward, whom his master will set over his household, to give them their portion of food at the proper time?'" (Luke 12:42).

Object:

A photograph or painting of cows and sheep grazing

Development:

There is an old nursery rhyme that goes:

> Little Boy Blue, come blow your horn;
> Sheep in the meadow, cows in the corn.
> Oh, where is the boy who looks after
>   the sheep?
> He's under a haystack, fast asleep!

Have you ever promised to do something, and then forgot or simply didn't get around to doing it?

In the rhyme, Little Boy Blue was supposed to watch the cows and the sheep, but instead he lay down and went to sleep. The cows he was told to watch got out of their pasture and went into a corn field, where they probably trampled and ruined a lot of corn. The sheep got out and went into a meadow.

When we fail to do what we said we would do, or fail to carry out jobs that have been assigned to us, we often hurt and disappoint other people.

Sometimes other people disappoint us, too. We rely on them for something, and when they don't do it, we feel bad.

The faithful and wise steward that the Bible talks about is the kind of person who can be counted on to carry out the job he is given. Each of us must try to be like that, so we don't hurt and disappoint those around us.

26

Follow the Leader

Text:

"Let them alone; they are blind guides. And if a blind man leads a blind man, both will fall into a pit" (Matt. 15:14).

Object:

Two handkerchiefs or towels to use as blindfolds

Development:

(Ask for two volunteers, and place a blindfold on each. Then ask one to follow the other for a short distance.)

What happens when two people can't see, and one tries to follow the other?

It's pretty easy for both to become lost, isn't it? As the Bible said, both are likely to fall into a pit.

(Remove children's blindfolds.)

Do you know how we might be like blind people following other blind people?

People who really are blind—those who physically can't see—still often live happy, productive, and meaningful lives. On the other hand, those who can see with their eyes but still are blinded by ignorance or temptation are much worse off, because they may let themselves stumble into trouble.

If someone were to try to get us to take drugs or alcohol, or maybe to get us to steal or tell lies, and if we did so, then it would be like letting a blind person lead us. The person trying to get us to do bad things is blind to the dangers, and we would be blind, too, if we followed them.

Even though we may be able to see, we must never allow ourselves to be tempted by others to engage in dangerous or unchristian activities.

27

Birds and Flowers

Text:

"Look at the birds of the air: they neither sow nor reap nor gather into barns, and yet your heavenly Father feeds them. Are you not of more value than they? . . . And why are you anxious about clothing? Consider the lilies of the field, how they grow; they neither toil nor spin; yet I tell you, even Solomon in all his glory was not arrayed like one of these" (Matt. 6:26, 28–29).

Objects:

Pictures of birds and flowers

Development:

Have you ever thought about all the beautiful things that God looks after in his world? There are millions of flowers, birds, trees, mountains, lakes, streams. Sometimes we forget how many of these beautiful things there are in the world.

How many birds and flowers, do you think, actually worry about whether or not they are beautiful?

Have you ever seen a worried bird, or a nervous flower?

But, all we humans have been worried and sometimes very nervous. And yet think of all the things we have to be thankful for, such as healthy bodies, good minds, parents, friends, homes, and other blessings.

When we get to worrying too much, God says we should remember the birds and the flowers. They don't worry at all, and yet they are more colorful and beautiful than the fanciest queens or kings.

28

The Great Stone Face

Text:

". . . looking to Jesus, the pioneer and perfecter of our faith, who for the joy that was set before him endured the cross, despising the shame, and is seated at the right hand of the throne of God" (Heb. 12:2).

Object:

A picture of the Great Stone Face

Development:

Near a place called Franconia Notch in the White Mountains of New Hampshire is a rock formation that looks surprisingly like a human face. People who live in the area call it the "Old Man of the Mountains." Many people come from long distances every year just to gaze at the mountainside and take pictures of the "face" formed by nature in the rock.

For many generations people have talked about the face and have told stories about it. One famous story, told more than a hundred years ago, was about a young boy who lived near the mountain and gazed nearly every day at the face in the rock.

The boy had often heard the legend that said someday a man whose face was just like the great stone face would come to the town. The boy watched and waited, but the man didn't come.

Finally, when the boy had long since become an old man, someone pointed at him and said that his face looked just like the great stone face. In looking at the rock so often, his face had taken on its characteristics.

What we think about the most each day helps to determine what kind of people we are becoming and what kinds of attitudes and values we carry through life. We need to think about Jesus and look to him often, so that we can grow to be like him.

29

All Equal

Text:

"There is neither Jew nor Greek, there is neither slave nor free, there is neither male nor female; for you are all one in Christ Jesus" (Gal. 3:28).

Objects:

All of the children present

Development:

Usually we use common objects to help with the children's sermon, but today the objects are very special. They are *you*.

Those of you who are boys know that there are some jobs or activities in life that boys and men like to do more often than girls or women do. Pro football, for example, is pretty much played by men. The same is true of big league baseball and some other activities. On the other hand, there are certain types of jobs, professions, sports, and other activities that girls and women are more likely to prefer.

It's fine when people follow their preferences and

do what they like best. In some parts of the world, however, people aren't given a choice. They are treated very differently because they are men or women, boys or girls. Women in some countries, for example, must wear veils over their faces, and in some places girls and women are treated like property to be "owned" by their husbands or fathers. This is bad, for just as it is wrong to be unkind to someone because of the color of his or her skin, so it is wrong to mistreat someone because they are male or because they are female.

Aren't we fortunate to live in a country where anyone can become almost anything he or she wishes, whether they are boys or girls? And even the Bible says this is a better way. Instead of male or female, the Bible says, we are all *one* in Christ Jesus.

30

My Secret Heart

Text:

"Behold, thou desirest truth in the inward being;
therefore teach me wisdom in my secret heart" (Ps.
51:6).

Object:

A locket with a secret compartment for a photo

Development:

Do you like secrets?

Can you keep a secret?

Sometimes secrets are the hardest things to keep
to ourselves. The fact that we aren't supposed to tell
anybody makes it very difficult not to tell.

Do you know that each of us has secrets, even
though we don't always think about them? It's true.
Because we are human, with lots of thoughts and
ideas and likes and dislikes and preferences and attitudes and hopes and dreams, there always will be
things inside us that no one else except God knows
about. God knows everything in our hearts, and he

loves us all—in spite of our secrets and innermost thoughts.

Because God can see into our hearts, we should ask him to guide us and give us direction in all we do. That's what the psalmist was asking in the text we listened to. He was asking God to teach him wisdom in the psalmist's "secret heart."

We should ask God to give us wisdom, too, in our secret hearts.

31

In Trouble

Text:

"When he calls to me, I will answer him; I will be with him in trouble, I will rescue him and honor him" (Ps. 91:15).

Object:

A picture of Batman or Superman

Development:

Have you ever been in trouble and wished Batman or Superman were there to help you?

Sometimes we get in trouble that isn't even our fault. Maybe we lose something, or something is stolen, or somebody bigger and stronger is mean to us.

Wouldn't it be fun to have a superhero friend who could lend us a hand, and maybe help us out of trouble, or at least help us to feel better and not worry?

Well, we have such a friend, but he isn't somebody with a cape or a funny costume or a weird car. He's God. God promises to be with us in all kinds of trouble if we only ask him. "I will be with him in trouble," says the psalm. "I will rescue him and honor him."

In God we have a real "superhero," instead of one made up from comic books and movies.

God is always there for us, no matter what problems come along and no matter how big the problems seem. All we need to do is talk to him and ask for his help.

32

A True Friend

Text:

"A true friend is always loyal, and a brother is born to help in time of need" (Prov. 17:17 LB).

Object:

A picture of two or more friends, arm-in-arm

Development:

Who is your best friend? (*Ask several of the children.*)

Do you think it's possible to have more than one best friend? What is your best friend like? (*Have a few children tell.*)

Does your best friend ever get mad at you? Chances are, he or she does, because it's pretty unusual for two people to always agree on everything. Do you ever get mad at your best friend?

What's the best thing we can do when someone, whether friend or not, does something to hurt our feelings or make us mad?

Jesus says we should forgive them. We should try

not to stay mad, but instead should try to get over it and not hold a grudge.

Do you know what the best thing is about a true friend? Most people would say it's *loyalty*. A true friend is loyal, no matter what happens. Even if you have fights, a true friend remains your friend. That's why the Bible verse for today says, "A true friend is always loyal."

Most of us would agree that friends, and best friends, are some of the most wonderful things on earth.

Let's bow our heads and say a short prayer together. The prayer is: "Thank you, God, for friends."

33

Pebbles

Text:

"And I will put this third into the fire, and refine them as one refines silver, and test them as gold is tested" (Zech. 13:9).

Objects:

A few shiny pebbles

Development:

Mica is a mineral—a part of many kinds of rocks—that is found in several countries of the earth. Have you ever seen mica in a pebble or a stone?

Maybe you don't know if you have seen mica or not, but there is one way to tell: Usually it is very shiny. Sometimes it looks like little flakes within the stone. Often it sparkles and looks like silver. However, mica isn't nearly as valuable as silver.

Another mineral that people have been fooled by is pyrite, which looks very much like gold. Therefore, pyrite is also known as "fool's gold."

If people test pyrite by the refiner's very hot fire, it will not melt the way gold does, and the difference between gold and pyrite becomes clear.

Sometimes God tests us by means of tough or difficult experiences, and sometimes we are tempted to do or say things that are contrary to what God would want us to do or say.

When we are tested in this way, we find out whether our faith is made of true gold or "fool's gold."

34

Letters

Text:

"You yourselves are our letter of recommendation, written on your hearts, to be known and read by all men; and you show that you are a letter from Christ delivered by us, written not with ink but with the Spirit of the living God, not on tablets of stone but on tablets of human hearts" (2 Cor. 3:2–3).

Objects:

A variety of used envelopes

Development:

What kind of letter, do you suppose, came in each of these envelopes?

(*Display envelopes as they're discussed.*)

Maybe this one had a check in it.

Perhaps this had junk mail or a catalog or an advertisement.

This could have been a birthday card, or maybe a letter from one friend to another.

How, do you think, did those who received these

envelopes react to them? Do you think they might have been happy to get them? Were they sad or angry?

In the Bible Paul called Christians "a letter from Christ."

We can be "letters" by being friends and showing kindness to the physically impaired, to persons with skin a different color than ours, or to the new kid in school. We can be a love "message" from God, regardless of where we are or with whom we happen to be.

What kind of "letter" are you?

35

Remembering

Text:

"Remember also your Creator in the days of your youth, before the evil days come, and the years draw nigh, when you will say, 'I have no pleasure in them'" (Eccles. 12:1).

Object:

A short piece of string

Development:

(Tie the string loosely around one child's finger.)

Do you all know what this is? That's right. It's just a simple piece of string. Years ago, people used to say that if you have something important to remember, you should tie a little piece of string like this around your finger. Later, the string will remind you of what it was you wanted to remember. But never make it tight, or it will make your finger sick and sore.

Are you good at remembering? Do you always remember to do your homework? Do you always remember promises you made to your mom or dad, or to your friends?

Some people have tremendous memories and can remember entire books, word-for-word. Other people can't remember what they had for breakfast this morning.

Several things help your memory. One is that if you work to develop a good memory when you are young, it will be easier to remember things when you are old.

The Bible reminds us that when we are young we should remember the God who made us, so that the days, and our memories, will be pleasant when we are old.

36

Good Fruit, Bad Fruit

Text:

"But the fruit of the Spirit is love, joy, peace, patience, kindness, goodness, faithfulness, gentleness, self-control; against such there is no law" (Gal. 5:22–23).

Object:

A lemon or other sour fruit, and an apple or other sweet fruit

Development:

Both of our objects today are fruit, but how different they are! Which do you prefer to eat—sour or sweet fruit? Most people, I think, prefer sweet fruit. Sour fruit makes you "pucker up" sometimes, causing you to make terrible faces when you eat it. And when fruit is spoiled, it tastes even worse.

Did you know that people often are like either sweet or sour fruit?

Some people are like sour fruit. They seem to be mean, ugly, quarrelsome, greedy, and generally nasty to the world around them.

Other people are like sweet fruit. They are like the people Paul talked about in the Bible verses today. They try to show and maintain love, joy, peace, patience, kindness, goodness, faithfulness, gentleness, and self-control. Paul calls these virtues the "fruit of the Spirit."

If we leave God out of our lives, we risk becoming like the "sour fruit" people, who go around feeling bad and making those around them feel bad, too.

If we pray and ask for God's help, however, we can have the fruit of the Spirit, just as the Bible says. In so doing, we will feel good about our world, and we will brighten the lives of those around us, too.

Which do you want to be like—sweet fruit or sour fruit?

37

Oaks and Acorns

Text:

"Another parable he put before them, saying, 'The kingdom of heaven is like a grain of mustard seed which a man took and sowed in his field; it is the smallest of all seeds, but when it has grown it is the greatest of shrubs and becomes a tree, so that the birds of the air come and make nests in its branches'" (Matt. 13:31–32).

Object:

An acorn or some other type of nut

Development:

Mustard seeds are pretty tiny and hard to see, so let's substitute a seed that's slightly larger. Do you know what this is? It's an acorn. Do you know what comes from acorns?

Well, it's hard to imagine, but from small acorns like this come giant oak trees that are many, many feet tall.

You were very tiny once, too. Have you ever

thought about what you will be like when you grow up? How tall will you be? Whom will you look like?

When you become a grown-up woman or man, it may seem hard to believe that you were once a tiny baby. Chances are, as a grownup you won't look much like you did when you were born.

Jesus told us that the kingdom of heaven is like a seed, too, and the world is like the field in which the seed grows. As more people love God and follow Jesus, the "seed" grows. The kingdom of heaven, like the mighty oak tree, grows larger and stronger the more we follow Jesus and grow in God's love.

Isn't it wonderful to be a part of this special seed?

38

You Are the Greatest

Text:

"At that time the disciples came to Jesus, saying, 'Who is the greatest in the kingdom of heaven?' And calling to him a child, he put him in the midst of them, and said, 'Truly, I say to you, unless you turn and become like children, you will never enter the kingdom of heaven'" (Matt. 18:1–3).

Objects:

All the children present

Development:

Most of the time, we have objects with our children's sermons, but today is different. Do you know what the objects are today? They're you, each one of the children here. I'll tell you why.

First, I'd like to ask you a question. Who do you think are the greatest people in our world? The president? Baseball or basketball or football heroes? Movie stars?

Lots of people have lots of opinions on that question. Many people think that the most important people in our world are the ones who are famous, or powerful, or rich, or especially skilled at doing something.

But do you want to know something interesting? People once asked Jesus who the greatest people were, and he didn't name a single rich or famous or powerful person. In Jesus' eyes, *children* are the greatest people in the world! He said everybody in the world, especially the grownups, have to be like children to get into heaven. Maybe that's because too many grownups have learned to do too many bad things by the time they grow up, or think they have nothing more to learn about Jesus' love.

So, remember Jesus' special love for children, and be sure to thank him for his love for you and for all of us.

39

Inside and Outside

Text:

"Woe to you, Pharisees, and you religious leaders—hypocrites! You are so careful to polish the outside of the cup, but the inside is foul with extortion and greed" (Matt. 23:25 LB).

Object:

A large cup that is clean on the outside but obviously dirty on the inside

Development:

(*Pass the cup around for each of the children to examine.*)

How often have you been told to wash your hands or take a bath or wash the dog or clean something else? Quite a few times? It's important to be clean.

We all know that staying clean on the outside is a pretty good idea, but what about the inside? I don't mean that we ought to try to swallow a bar of soap! But how about what comes into our minds and hearts? In our Bible reading today, Jesus became angry with people who worked hard to look clean and polished on the outside, but inside they were still filled with greed and sin and bad thoughts.

How do we stay clean on the inside?

God can help us. If we pray and ask for his help, he can help us to think pure thoughts, and to get rid of the pettiness and greed and envy and hatreds that make us dirty on the inside—even though our outsides may be perfectly polished and clean.

40

Doing Good

Text:

"And the King will answer them, 'Truly, I say to you, as you did it to one of the least of these my brethren, you did it to me'" (Matt. 25:40).

Object:

A picture of a small shop, or a shoemaker at work

Development:

A folk tale from long ago tells of a devout shopkeeper, perhaps a shoemaker, who had only one wish: to see Jesus. Each night he prayed and asked if somehow he could see the Lord.

Finally one night, a message came to him during his prayers. A voice said, "I will visit you tomorrow."

The next day he was very excited as he went to his shop. While he worked and waited, a widow and her child came in and asked for food, for it was cold outside and they had nothing to eat. The shopkeeper gave them some food.

Later, while he was still waiting, an old man, who looked very cold, walked by, and the shopkeeper invited him in to get warm.

Still later, others came by, and the shopkeeper was kind to them all. But he was very disappointed that Jesus had not come into the shop. In his prayers that night, he expressed his disappointment about not seeing the Lord, after having been promised that he would come.

"I *did* come to you," said a voice from above. "*I* was the hungry woman and child. *I* was the old man to whom you offered warmth. So you shall be blessed for your kindness and mercy."

Do you think Jesus sometimes appears to us as a poor beggar? As someone sad or lonely? As someone in need?

How would you treat such people?

41

God's Vision

Text:

"Search me, O God, and know my heart! Try me and know my thoughts!" (Ps. 139:23).

". . . because he knew all men and needed no one to bear witness of man; for he himself knew what was in man" (John 2:25).

Object:

Radiograph (x-ray), or photo of an x-ray negative

Development:

Many people have x-rays taken when they go to visit the doctor or dentist. Have any of you ever had an x-ray taken?

When you get an x-ray, a special machine takes a "picture" of a portion of your body. You don't feel it, but the machine is able to send rays through you and show bone and other material inside your body. When the doctor thinks you may have broken a bone, for example, the x-ray shows whether or not there is a break and where it is if there is one. X-rays show dentists if teeth are coming in or if you have cavities.

X-rays, then, permit doctors to "look" inside us without opening us up.

As good as x-rays are, there is something that is better and can look farther inside us. Do you know what that is?

It's God's vision.

God has what we might call a "divine x-ray" that lets him know exactly what is inside us—whether good or bad.

Because God can see inside us at all times, we should pray as the psalmist did in our text, asking God to look inside our hearts and show us how to live the best lives we can, all the time.

42

The Same Forever

Text:

"Jesus Christ is the same yesterday and today and forever" (Heb. 13:8).

Object:

A picture of a baby

Development:

Have you seen a picture of yourself when you were a baby? Chances are, you looked a lot different from how you look today. And chances are, you look quite a bit different today than you will several years from now after you have become adults.

Have you ever looked closely at a friend of yours, and wondered what he or she will look like as a grandpa or grandma?

Have you ever seen a picture of your grandpa or grandma as a baby? It's even harder to imagine that the grandparents we know today once looked so different.

Things are changing all the time in our lives. The

friends we have today may not be the same friends we have next year, or maybe even next month. Sometimes we change schools or grades or the towns we live in. Sometimes we change houses or get different teachers.

Some changes are happy, such as when we move into a new house or gain a new friend. And some changes are sad, such as when someone we know dies, or a friend moves away, or we lose a pet.

Sometimes it seems as though almost everything in life changes at one time or another. In fact, everything does change.

The Bible tells us that there is something, though, that never, ever changes, and that is Jesus Christ. We should be very grateful, for, as the Bible says, he is the same yesterday, today, and forever.

43

The Whole World

Text:

"For God so loved the world that he gave his only Son, that whoever believes in him should not perish but have eternal life" (John 3:16).

Object:

A globe

Development:

There is an old chorus that goes like this (*use with music if possible*):

> Jesus loves the little children,
> All the children of the world;
> Red and yellow, black and white,
> All are precious in his sight;
> Jesus loves the little children
> of the world.

Sometimes it seems as though this old world could almost split into pieces because of all the war and hatred and trouble. Christians, Jew, Islamics, communists, noncommunists, and many others seem to be at odds with each other every day in some part of the world.

With all the trouble, though, we must always remember something: God loves the whole world—not just this part or that part. And God loved the world so much, the Bible tells us, that he gave his only Son, so that everyone who believes in him might have eternal life.

We need to remember this always, and remember especially that all of us are God's children—whether our skin is red, yellow, brown, black, or white—and that God loves us all.

44

Of What Are You Afraid?

Text:

> "Fear not, for I am with you,
>   be not dismayed, for I am your God;
> I will strengthen you, I will
>   help you,
> I will uphold you with my victorious
>   right hand" (Isa. 41:10).

Object:

Rubber snake or spider

Development:

(Pass object around for the children to examine.)

Are you glad this is only a rubber snake (or spider)? If it were real, would you be afraid?

What are some of the things that you are most afraid of? *(Ask for examples.)*

We all know of things that frighten us. And some things that frighten one person aren't frightening at all to someone else.

Fright can be a very good thing. Do you know why? For one thing, if we were never afraid, we easily could walk into all kinds of trouble and get hurt. What if we were not afraid of rattlesnakes or grizzly bears? What would happen?

Those are real fears that help to protect us. Some of our fears, though, turn out to be only in our imaginations. How many of you have seen something you thought was frightening, and it turned out to be no more than a shadow?

Whatever our fears, we need to remember the words that God gave to Isaiah in the Bible: "Fear not, for I am with you." God is with us *all the time.* If we can remember that, then most of our silly fears will vanish.

45

Whom Do You Obey?

Text:

"But Peter and the apostles answered, 'We must obey God rather than men'" (Acts 5:29).

Object:

Picture of parent with child, or classroom situation

Development:

Whom do you obey?

Your mom or dad? What would happen if your mother or father told you to do something, and you said no?

What about your teacher in school? Does she or he make you obey? What if your teacher told you to do something, and you said you weren't going to because you simply didn't feel like it? Would the teacher be likely to say, "Fine, do whatever you wish," or would you end up being punished?

We obey moms and dads and teachers and police officers and some others because we have learned that, whether we like it or not, they usually tell us to do things that we should do, things that are for our benefit or safety.

If a stranger told you to walk in front of a speeding train, however, you probably wouldn't obey.

So sometimes we have to decide whom we will obey.

When Peter was told by authorities that he should stop preaching about Jesus, Peter was forced to make that type of decision. Peter knew that he must follow his heart and his conscience rather than the orders of people who hated Jesus. So he refused to obey. Instead, he told them, "We must obey God rather than men."

We should pray to God and ask for his help in making the right decisions. Ask him to help us to know when we should obey orders and when we shouldn't.

46

The "Home" Church

Text:

". . . greet also the church in their house" (Rom. 16:5a).

Object:

Picture of a house

Development:

Did you know that the first Christians had no church buildings like the one in which we now sit? They had no choirs, no pianos or organs, no Sunday schools, no pews, no hymn books, no buildings, and no one like me standing in front of them.

The first groups of Christians met in people's homes. It was the only place they could be together to pray and have fellowship in peace.

Today, some Christian groups still meet only in homes—not in churches.

While it is wonderful to have a church in which to worship, we must not forget that a church is not the only place in which people can worship God. At home, every time we pray or say grace before a meal, we're having a form of church. Any time we pray or read our Bibles at home, we are in a sense having church.

That doesn't mean that we want to get rid of this building and simply worship at home. What it does mean, though, is that we shouldn't think that church, and worship, are things we participate in and do only once a week in just one building we happen to call church.

Our worship and the expression of our love of God should never be restricted by buildings and locations. We can love and worship God, and talk to him and be guided by him, wherever we happen to be.

47

Thanksgiving

Text:

"Bless the LORD, O my soul;
and all that is within me,
bless his holy name!
Bless the LORD, O my soul,
  and forget not all his benefits,
who forgives all your iniquity,
  who heals all your diseases,
who redeems your life from the Pit,
  who crowns you with steadfast
    love and mercy,
who satisfies you with good as long
  as you live
    so that your youth is renewed like
the eagle's" (Ps. 103:1–5).

Object:

Picture of Pilgrims and Indians at the first Thanksgiving

Development:

More than three hundred years ago the Pilgrims and Indians gathered for a thanksgiving feast. The

Pilgrims were thankful to God for bringing them through their first year in the new country, for the freedom to worship in their own way, and for the Indians who had helped them with planting their crops. Though the winter had been extremely difficult and many Pilgrims had died, the survivors had now harvested their first crops.

Long before the Pilgrims came to America, the psalmist in the Bible was thankful, too, for all the blessings from God.

Today, as we think about Thanksgiving, we should remind ourselves of all the things we have, and we should say a prayer of thanks to God, just as the Pilgrims and the psalmist did.

What are you thankful for?

48

Your Two Bodies

Text:

"It is sown a physical body, it is raised a spiritual body. If there is a physical body, there is also a spiritual body" (1 Cor. 15:44).

Objects:

Some seeds

Development:

Have you ever helped someone plant a garden? If you have, you know that seeds must be planted for anything to grow.

It's exciting to wait and watch as the tiny shoots begin to show at the surface of the earth and then rise to become vegetables and flowers.

In some ways, it's a miracle. Inside each seed is a "spark" of life. Under the right conditions, it grows and expands and becomes what it was meant to be, while the outer shell of the seed falls off and decays in the earth.

If we think about it, we can see that we, as children of God, are very much like the seeds. Our bodies are like the shell of the seed that carries the spark of life, and of God, deep inside. Our physical bodies live perhaps eighty years or more, and then are cast away when we die. Inside us, however, is the soul that God gave us (like the spark of life in the seed), and that soul continues to live forever.

It is the soul that the Bible talks about when it says there is a spiritual body as well as a physical body. And with this miracle God has given us, we know that we truly will never die.

49

Thy Word in My Heart

Text:

"I have laid up thy word in my heart, that I might not sin against thee" (Ps. 119:11).

Objects:

A heart-shaped candy box containing a small Bible

Development:

Many people have memorized prayers, and they still can remember them. For example, do you have a special table grace that you say before meals? Sometimes people learn a good-night prayer, such as "Now I lay me down to sleep," when they are small children, and they still remember it when they are grown up.

Do any of you know the Lord's Prayer? (*Optional: Repeat Lord's Prayer with the children.*)

Is anyone familiar with John 3:16? (*Optional: Read verse to children.*)

How about the twenty-third psalm? (*Optional: Read Psalm 23 to children.*)

Learning and memorizing passages from the Bible helps us to be more aware of God. It not only helps us to lead better lives, but these prayers and verses will comfort us in the future as we keep them in our hearts.

50

The Big Parade

Text:

"Suddenly, the angel was joined by a vast host of others—the armies of heaven—praising God: 'Glory to God in the highest heaven,' they sang, 'and peace on earth for all those pleasing him'" (Luke 2:13–14 LB).

Object:

A picture of angels and shepherds

Development:

Have you ever watched a parade? Maybe you've seen the Tournament of Roses parade or a Thanksgiving parade on television, or maybe you've seen another parade. Have you ever been in a parade? It is very exciting to walk or ride down the center of a street and see all the people waving from the sidelines.

Parades are happy events, because everyone seems to be celebrating and enjoying the occasion.

Do you remember what happened on the night Jesus was born? The Bible tells us that shepherds near Bethlehem saw many angels in the sky—something like a parade of them—and they were all singing praises to God because Jesus was born.

What a glorious moment that must have been! What a wonderful thing it must have been for the shepherds to see a huge "parade" of angels, all singing and celebrating! It was as though all of heaven and earth were happy at once because of that very special birth.

This is why we like to celebrate Christ's birth each year. We are still thankful and still singing praises to God for sending his Son to save us and give us eternal life.

51

Christmas

Text:

"For to us a child is born,
    to us a son is given;
and the government will be upon
        his shoulder,
    and his name will be called
'Wonderful Counselor,
    Mighty God,
    Everlasting Father, Prince of
        Peace'" (Isa. 9:6).

Object:

A toy cradle with a doll in it

Development:

Hundreds of years before Jesus was born in Bethlehem, the prophet Isaiah talked about a baby that would be born, a baby that would come to be called the Prince of Peace. The prophet was right. He accurately predicted the birth of Jesus.

It's a very special day when a baby is born. Do any of you have little brothers or sisters? Do you remember when they were born? When you were born, it was a very special day, too. Your parents, grandparents, and maybe other people, too, were very happy on that day.

When Jesus was born, it was a special day for Joseph and Mary, but it was also much more. Jesus, as the son of God, was sent by God to bring his message of love and forgiveness to all people. That made his birth more than just important. It was the most important birth in all of history.

God gave us his son, many years ago in Bethlehem, so that we all may have everlasting life. On this day, and every day throughout the year, we should thank God for the birth of the baby Jesus.

52

Your Body, a Temple of God

Text:

"Do you not know that your body is a temple of the Holy Spirit within you, which you have from God? You are not your own; you were bought with a price. So glorify God in your body" (1 Cor. 6:19–20).

Object:

A toy church, or a picture of a church

Development:

How many things can you spot right here, in the building where we're sitting, that are designed to remind us of God's presence?

The cross certainly reminds us of God, doesn't it? What other symbols do you see? (*Point to objects as they're mentioned.*) There are candles, flowers, pictures, stained-glass windows, the Christian flag, the altar. All of these things, and more, remind us of God and help us to focus on him in our worship. You could say that these are the things that make a church the home of God, don't you think?

In the Bible, Paul tells us that our bodies are like churches or temples, too. They are places where God lives, for he is always in us. Because our bodies are temples of the Holy Spirit, Paul reminds us that they, in a sense, aren't really ours alone, but belong to God. Therefore, we should treat our bodies as we would treat God's home.

That means that we shouldn't hurt our bodies. We must remember this when someone wants us to take drugs or do other things that could hurt our bodies. Just as we wouldn't take harmful things into church, so we shouldn't let them into our bodies where God also lives.

Scripture Index

Subject Index